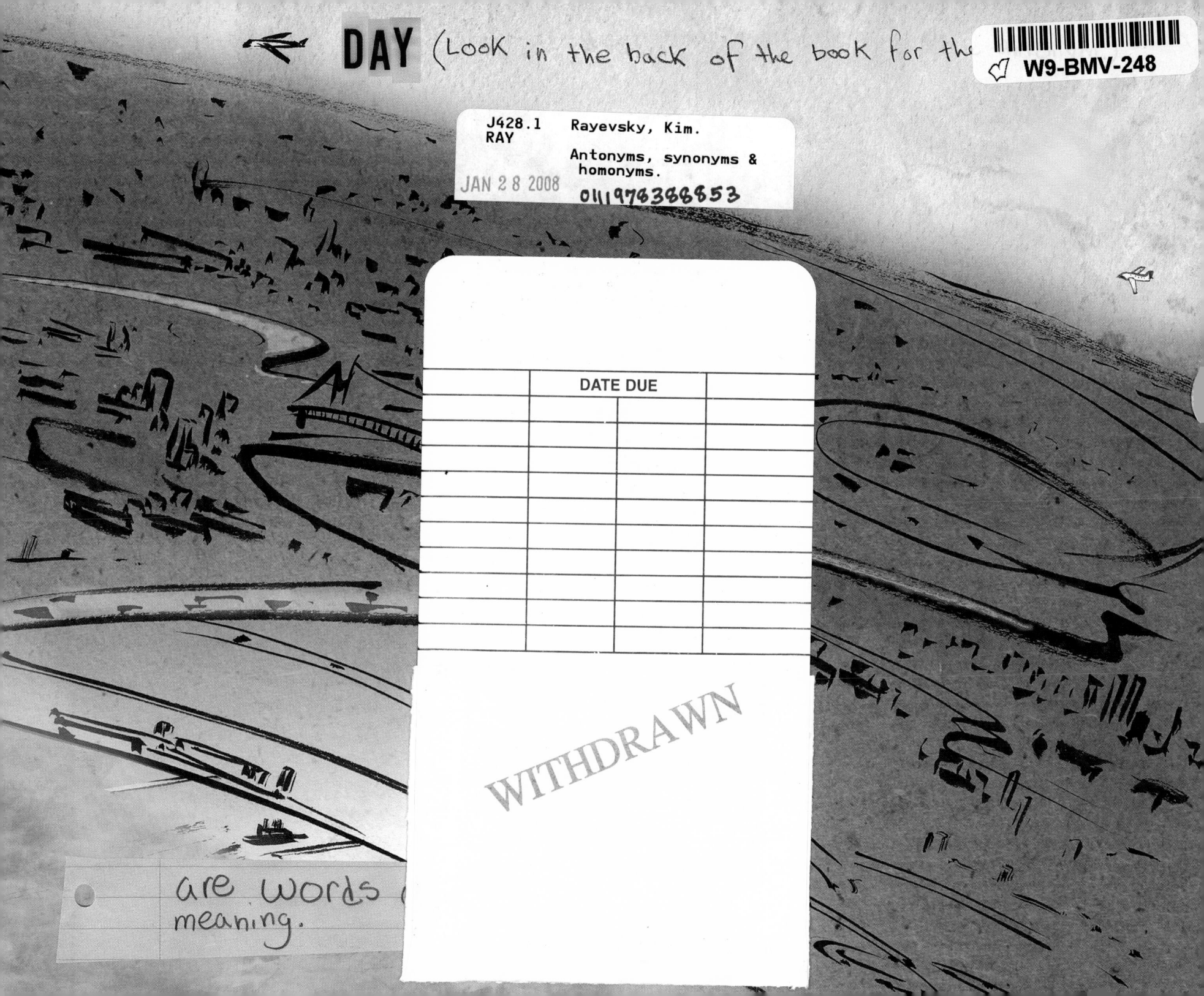

W9-BMV-248

J428.1 Rayevsky, Kim.
RAY
Antonyms, synonyms & homonyms.
JAN 28 2008
0111976388853

DATE DUE

WITHDRAWN

INSIDE
FARTHER FROM
LEFT PAGE
ANTONYMS,
SYNONYMS
& HOMONYMS
cowardly

by Kim & Robert Rayevsky

HOLIDAY HOUSE / NEW YORK

CLEAN
DIRTY

NICE
SMILE
NAUGHTY

horisontal wrong spelling
horizontal RIGHT spelling
spread

NEAT

high UP

DEEP
DOWN

ANTONYMS

ON THE TOP OF THE BUILDING
UNDER the mattresses
FRIENDLY
HOSTILE
FULL
EMPTY
REAL ANIMALS
ugly
Marcel Duchamp
Mona Lisa, 1919
Beautiful
Leonardo da Vinci
Mona Lisa, 1503-6
awake
alert
asleep
UNCOLORED - - - - - - - - - - BLACK - - and - - WHITE - - PICTURES
Fantastic, MYTHOLOGICAL ANIMAL
BIG
HUGE
little
small
tiny
HATTED
HATLESS
standing
sitting
LONELINESS
COMPANIONSHIP
OBEDIENT-DISOBEDIENT

GIVE
HAPPY BIRTHDAY
HAPPY BIRTHDAY
TAKE
COLD
HOT
safety
DARK background
LIGHT background
DANGER!!!
FEMALE SYMBOL
MALE SYMBOL
WOMAN
MAN
casual
dressed down
Dressed up
BEARDED
beardless
small beard
medium-sized beard
BIG beard
COLORED PICTURES
FULL
HUNGRY!!!
ABSTRACT PICTURE
realistic picture
surrealistic picture
underweight
lean
skinny
slim
slender
FAT
overweight

SYNONYMS

are different words that have the same meaning.

VEHICLE
WHEELS
car

MUSIC
MELODY
COMPOSITION
tune
song

TWO
of us are
WET.
DRENCHED
SOAKED
dripping
Sopping
I'm WET. I'm WET, TOO.
while singing in the rain!

HOUSE
HOME
road
street
bug insect
SYNONYMS
LARGE
tremendous
See
LOOK
WATCH
thorny
bristly
pretty handsome
attractive beautiful
pleasing
Seafood
prickly
spiny
Sharp
abominable
repulsive
repugnant
disgusting
DETESTABLE
abhorrent
HIDEOUS
SCARED
afraid
shocked
terrified
chilled
FRIGHTENED
ARCHITECTURE
structure
building
construction
Synonyms
teacher
professor

HUGE
beast
monster
GIANT
FISH
LITTLE
tiny
bounds
VAULTS
hurdles
SPRINGS
bounces
Jumps
leaps
Laugh
giggle
titter
Chuckle
SKETCHES
Doodles
drawings
teenager
ADOLESCENT
YOUTH
AMITY
tranquility
PEACE
HARMONY
CONCORD
UNITY
UNION
friendship
truce

I no longer SEE the SEA
as I fly my PLANE over the PLAIN.

HOMONYMS
are words that have the same sound and sometimes the same spelling, but different meanings.

I HEAR music, so HERE I am
all dressed up for the party.

WHERE'S
my hat?
My puppy WEARS
my hat!

school bus
TOW a bus with a TOE
I MISSED my mommy!

I ate a WHOLE doughnut and left only the HOLE.
The cat MISSED a mouse.

HOMONYMS
I SEW my pants.
I'm SO HAPPY!
I SAW WOOD. WOULD you help me?
Our camping SITE is out of SIGHT.
The Holiday House webSITE is:
WWW.holidayhouse.com
Window PANE
I SOW seeds.
It RAINS. the King REIGNS.
These FOUR cupcakes are FOR me!
I SAW a crocodile.
METE
BOAR
CANADA
USA
Nice to MEET you.
FORE!
He is a BORE.
MEAT
Ouch, I'm in PAIN!
THEY'RE THERE on THEIR boat.
Less flame!
My STEAK on a STAKE is at STAKE.

IDYLL
The NEW car is in IDLE.
I'm on my WAY TO adventures.
I'm on my WAY TO adventures, TOO.
you WEIGH TOO much.
Portland is the MAIN city in MAINE.
IDOL
WHERE?
I KNEW a GNU on Earth.
I proudly WEAR my hat.
$20.00
SELL this CELL phone for $20.00.
The TWO of them are WAY TOO adventurous!
He TRACKS the TRACKS along the TRACKS.
ceramic WARE
gnu
DOUGH
DOUGH
flute made from REED
RED balloon
DOE
I READ every night.

NIGHT

Text copyright © 2006 by Kim Rayevsky
Illustrations copyright © 2006 by Robert Rayevsky
Design by Robert and Kim Rayevsky
The mixed media artwork was created using pen, brush and ink, watercolor, acrylic, collage, coffee-stained paper, and other techniques including digital.
All Rights Reserved
Printed in the United States of America
www.holidayhouse.com
First Edition
1 3 5 7 9 10 8 6 4 2

Library of Congress Cataloging-in-Publication Data
Rayevsky, Kim.
Antonyms, synonyms, & homonyms / by Kim and Robert Rayevsky.—1st ed.
p. cm.
ISBN-13: 978-0-8234-1889-3 (hardcover)
ISBN-10: 0-8234-1889-8 (hardcover)
1. English language—Synonyms and antonyms—Juvenile literature.
2. English language—Homonyms—Juvenile literature. I. Rayevsky, Robert.
II. Title.

PE1591.R39 2006
428.1—dc22
2005035846

The image of Leonardo Da Vinci's *Mona Lisa* is used with permission of Harley Hahn at www.harley.com.

The image of Marcel Duchamp's *Mona Lisa LHOOQ* is used with permission of © 2006 Artists Rights Society (ARS), New York / ADAGP, Paris / Succession Marcel Duchamp.

The image of Charlie Chaplin is used with permission of the Roy Export Company Establishment.